Made in the USA
Las Vegas, NV
22 January 2021

16363099R00056